Oxford Reading Tree

Level 2

Floppy's Phonics

Activity Book

2

Debbie Hepplewhite

OXFORD

Say the sounds

j	v	w

-x	y	z

-zz	qu	ch

sh	th	th	-ng

-dge	-ve	wh

-cks	-tch	-nk

Practise the sound

Say the sound. Trace the letter.

Say the word. Listen for the /j/ sound.

jug   jet   jam   jig   jab   jog

Jill   Jack   just   jump   jets

jacket   juggle   jet lag   jumble

Sound out and blend to read the words.

 j   j   j

Say the sound. Trace the letters. Write the letters.

Say the words. When can you hear the /j/ sound?

Draw something beginning with **j**.

h   b   f   -ff   l   -ll   -le   -ss   **j**

2

Practise your reading and writing

Spell and write words with the focus grapheme.

1. Jess and Jill get on a jet.

2. Jack stuffs a jam bun in his jacket.

Blend to read the words and sentences.

Copy one of the sentences while saying the sounds of the words. Draw a picture to match the sentence.

Practise the sound

Say the sound. Trace the letter.

Say the word. Listen for the /v/ sound.

vet   van   Vic   vest   Val   van

vivid   vent   vans   vets   vest

visit   Kevin   velvet   invent

Sound out and blend to read the words.

 V   V   V   V

Say the sound. Trace the letters. Write the letters.

Say the words. When can you hear the /v/ sound?

Draw something beginning with **v**.

 b   f   -ff   l   -ll   -le   -ss   j   v

Practise your reading and writing

Spell and write words with the focus grapheme.

1. Val is a vet and she has seven pets.

2. Vic has a big red van and a red vest.

Blend to read the words and sentences.

Copy one of the sentences while saying the sounds of the words. Draw a picture to match the sentence.

Practise the sound

Say the sound. Trace the letter.

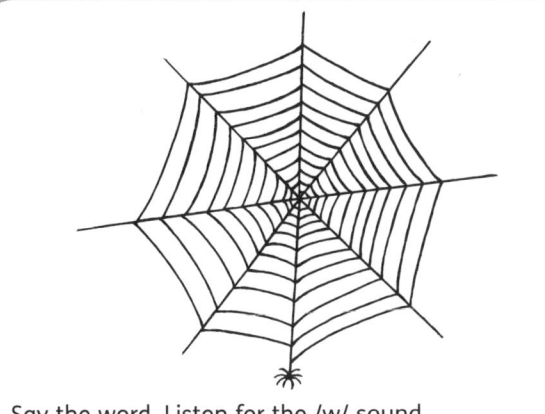

Say the word. Listen for the /w/ sound.

win   wag   web   will   win

wet   well   went   wags   webs

west   swim   wiggle   cobweb

Sound out and blend to read the words.

Say the sound. Trace the letters. Write the letters.

Say the words. When can you hear the /w/ sound?

Draw something beginning with **w**.

f   -ff   l   -ll   -le   -ss   j   v   **w**

Practise your reading and writing

Spell and write words with the focus grapheme.

1. If the wet dog wags, we will get wet.

2. Will got on a bus and went west.

Blend to read the words and sentences.

Copy one of the sentences while saying the sounds of the words. Draw a picture to match the sentence.

Practise the sound

Say the sound. Trace the letter.

Say the word. Listen for the /ks/ sound.

fix ox wax box tax cox

six Max mix fox six oxen

foxes text vixen next toxic

Sound out and blend to read the words.

Say the sound. Trace the letters. Write the letters.

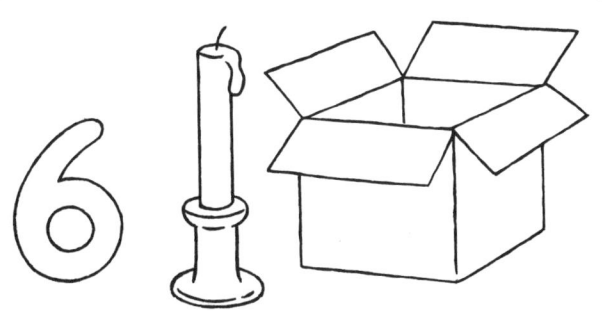

Say the words. When can you hear the /ks/ sound?

Draw something ending in **x**.

 -ff l -ll -le -ss j v w -**x**

Practise your reading and writing

Spell and write words with the focus grapheme.

1. The fox is in a fix as the ox is on his box.

2. The fox and the ox trod on the big black box.

Blend to read the words and sentences.

Copy one of the sentences while saying the sounds of the words. Draw a picture to match the sentence.

Practise the sound

Say the sound. Trace the letter.

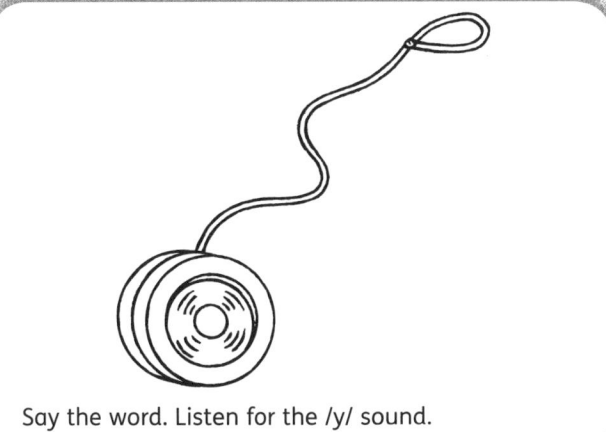

Say the word. Listen for the /y/ sound.

yes yap yet yam yell yak

yip yells yelp yaps yuck

yum yen Yasmin

Sound out and blend to read the words.

y y y y

Say the sound. Trace the letters. Write the letters.

Say the words. When can you hear the /y/ sound?

Draw something beginning with **y**.

 l -ll -le -ss j v w -x **y**

10

Practise your reading and writing

Spell and write words with the focus grapheme.

1. Yes, Yasmin, you can visit Vic.

2. The big yak's yells will not stop!

Blend to read the words and sentences.

Copy one of the sentences while saying the sounds of the words. Draw a picture to match the sentence.

Practise the sound

Say the sound. Trace the letter.

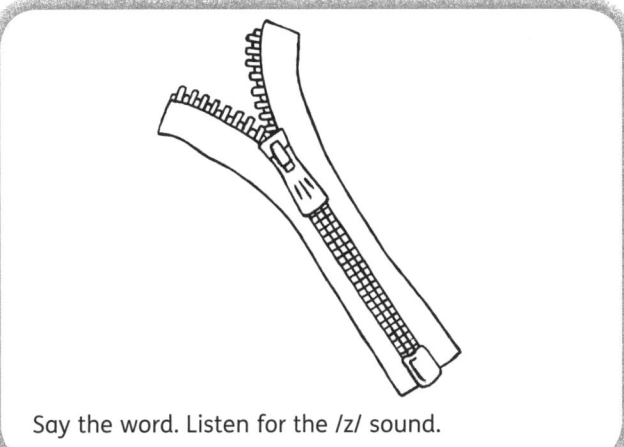

Say the word. Listen for the /z/ sound.

zip zap zit zinc zigzag

zips zaps zest Liz zebra

Zak zigzags zebras

Sound out and blend to read the words.

z z z z

Say the sound. Trace the letters. Write the letters.

Say the words. When can you hear the /z/ sound?

Draw something beginning with **z**.

 -ll -le -ss j v w -x y z

Practise your reading and writing

Spell and write words with the focus grapheme.

1. Zap is a little zigzag bug.

2. Biff went to see Zigzag and Zip, the zebras.

Blend to read the words and sentences.

Copy one of the sentences while saying the sounds of the words. Draw a picture to match the sentence.

Practise the sound

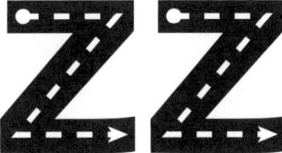

Say the sound. Trace the letters.

Say the word. Listen for the /z/ sound.

buzz   fizz   jazz   fuzz   buzz

puzzle   fizzle   muzzle   puzzles

razzle-dazzle   drizzle   grizzle

Sound out and blend to read the words.

zz   zz   zz   zz

Say the sound. Trace the letters. Write the letters.

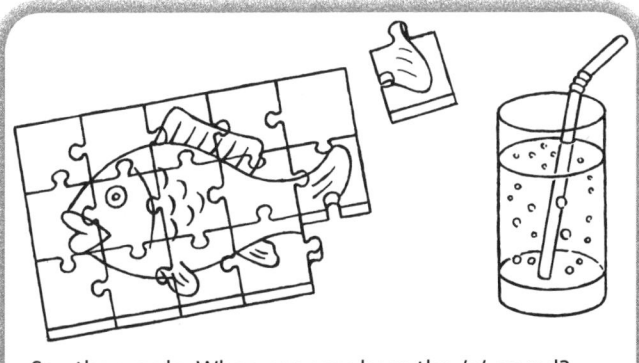

Say the words. When can you hear the /z/ sound?

Draw something ending with **zz**.

-le   -ss   j   v   w   -x   y   z   -zz

Practise your reading and writing

Spell and write words with the focus grapheme.

1. Six bugs zip and zap. They fuzz and buzz!

2. It was a big buzz, fizz, fizzle and fuss at the back of the bus.

Blend to read the words and sentences.

Copy one of the sentences while saying the sounds of the words. Draw a picture to match the sentence.

Practise the sound

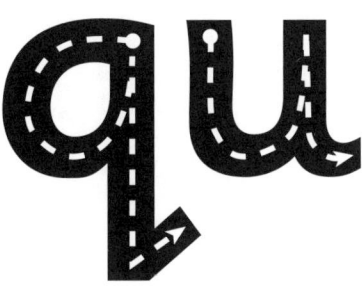

Say the sound. Trace the letters.

Say the word. Listen for the /kw/ sound.

quick   quit   quack   quest

quiff   quilt   quiz   quill

squid   squint   liquid

Sound out and blend to read the words.

qu   qu   qu   qu

Say the sound. Trace the letters. Write the letters.

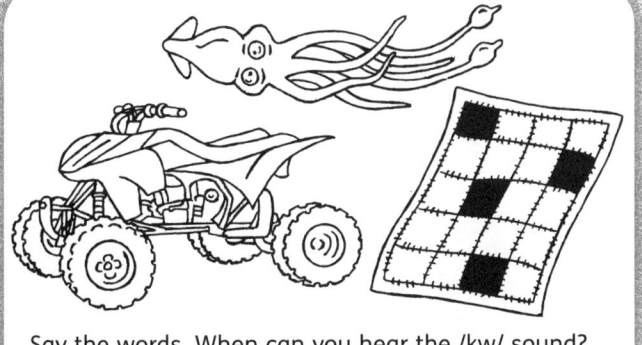

Say the words. When can you hear the /kw/ sound?

Draw something beginning with **qu**.

-ss   j   v   w   -x   y   z   -zz   **qu**

16

Spell and write words with the focus grapheme.

1. Quick! The duck can quack and peck!

2. She was quick but she quit the quiz.

Blend to read the words and sentences.

Copy one of the sentences while saying the sounds of the words. Draw a picture to match the sentence.

Practise the sound

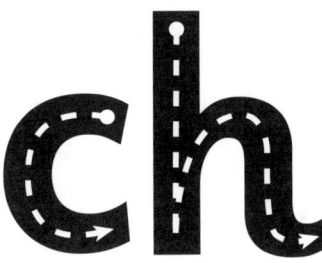

Say the sound. Trace the letters.

Say the word. Listen for the /ch/ sound.

chat   chin   chick   much

chips   rich   chop   chill   chess

check   lunch   munch   squelch

Sound out and blend to read the words.

ch   ch   ch   ch

Say the sound. Trace the letters. Write the letters.

Say the words. When can you hear the /ch/ sound?

Draw something beginning with **ch**.

j   v   w   -x   y   z   -zz   qu   **ch**

Practise your reading and writing

Spell and write words with the focus grapheme.

1. Chip had chips to munch on at lunch.

2. Chop up all the logs, and get the lunch.

Blend to read the words and sentences.

Copy one of the sentences while saying the sounds of the words. Draw a picture to match the sentence.

Practise the sound

Say the sound. Trace the letters.

Say the word. Listen for the /sh/ sound.

shop   shed   shut   fish   ship

shall   dish   shells   shock

wish   hush   shops   brush

Sound out and blend to read the words.

sh sh sh sh

Say the sound. Trace the letters. Write the letters.

Say the words. When can you hear the /sh/ sound?

Draw something beginning with **sh**.

w   -x   y   z   -zz   qu   ch   **sh**

Practise your reading and writing

Spell and write words with the focus grapheme.

1. She shuts her shell and she has her wish.

2. We must get off the ship and collect shells to
sell in the fish shop.

Blend to read the words and sentences.

Copy one of the sentences while saying the sounds of the words. Draw a picture to
match the sentence.

Practise the sound

Say the two sounds. Trace the letters.

Say the words 'this thumb'.

thin   thick   moth   maths

the   with   this   that   then

than   them   thud   thrill

Sound out and blend to read the words.

th   th   th   th

Say the two sounds. Trace the letters. Write the letters.

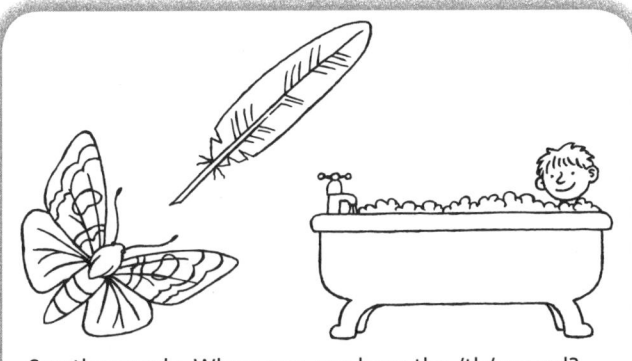

Say the words. When can you hear the /th/ sound?

Draw something ending in **th**.

-x   y   z   -zz   qu   ch   sh   **th**

Practise your reading and writing

Spell and write words with the focus grapheme.

1. Get a cloth that is thick, not thin.

2. I must get that thick cloth to mop up this froth.

Blend to read the words and sentences.

Copy one of the sentences while saying the sounds of the words. Draw a picture to match the sentence.

Practise the sound

Say the sound. Trace the letters.

Say the word. Listen for the /ng/ sound.

song   bang   wing   long

hang   thing   gong   rings

swing   lungs   bring   ping-pong

Sound out and blend to read the words.

ng   ng   ng   ng

Say the sound. Trace the letters. Write the letters.

Say the words. When can you hear the /ng/ sound?

Draw something ending in **ng**.

z   -zz   qu   ch   sh   th   -ng

Practise your reading and writing

Spell and write words with the focus grapheme.

1. The king sings and the bells go ding-dong.

2. Bring me a ring and I will sing to the king.

Blend to read the words and sentences.

Copy one of the sentences while saying the sounds of the words. Draw a picture to match the sentence.

Practise the sound

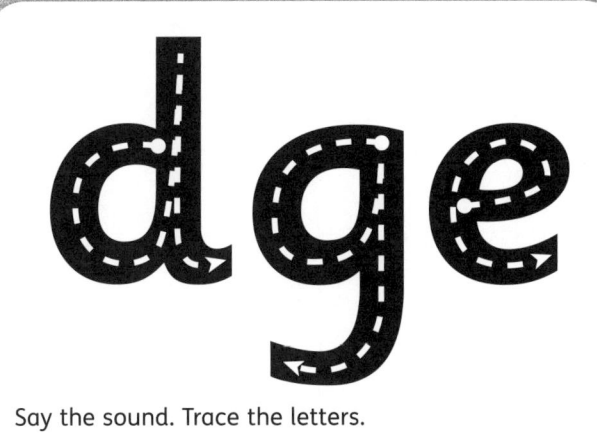

Say the sound. Trace the letters.

Say the word. Listen for the /j/ sound.

jam jug jet just jump jog

hedge badge judge edge

sludge midges fridge bridge

Sound out and blend to read the words. Some words revise **j** and other words practise **dge**.

dge dge dge

Say the sound. Trace the letters. Write the letters.

Say the words. When can you hear the /j/ sound?

Draw something ending in **dge**.

qu ch sh th -ng -**dge**

Practise your reading and writing

Spell and write words with the focus grapheme.

1. We all jog along the bridge.

2. Stand on the bridge and judge as the frogs

jump into the pond.

Blend to read the words and sentences.

Copy one of the sentences while saying the sounds of the words. Draw a picture to match the sentence.

Practise the sound

Say the sound. Trace the letters.

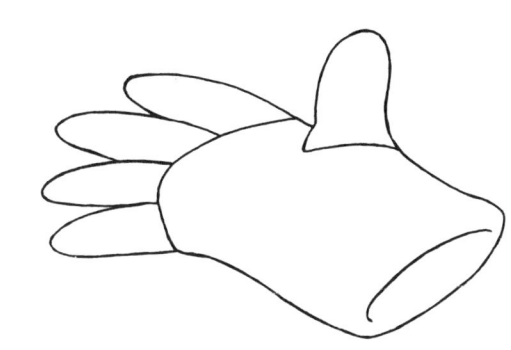

Say the word. Listen for the /v/ sound.

van   vet   vest   invent   Vic

have   give   live   l<u>o</u>ve   gives

d<u>o</u>ve   ab<u>o</u>ve   gl<u>o</u>ves   shelves

Sound out and blend to read the words. Some words revise **v** and other words practise **ve**.

Say the sound. Trace the letters. Write the letters.

Say the words. When can you hear the /v/ sound?

Draw something ending in **ve**.

ch sh th -ng -dge **-ve**

Practise your reading and writing

Spell and write words with the focus grapheme.

1. He lives in a big red van.

2. The vets have lost a van. Can you help them to solve the problem?

Blend to read the words and sentences.

Copy one of the sentences while saying the sounds of the words. Draw a picture to match the sentence.

Practise the sound

Say the sound. Trace the letters.

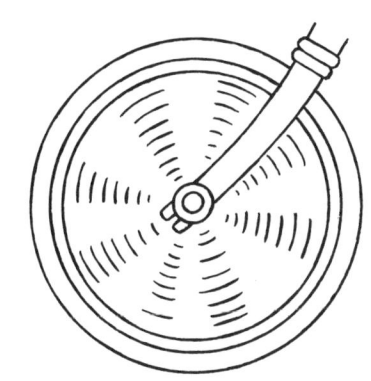

Say the word. Listen for the /w/ sound.

wet win will went wig

well west wagon wobble

when whisk whiff whizz

Sound out and blend to read the words. Some words revise **w** and other words practise **wh**.

wh wh wh wh

Say the sound. Trace the letters. Write the letters.

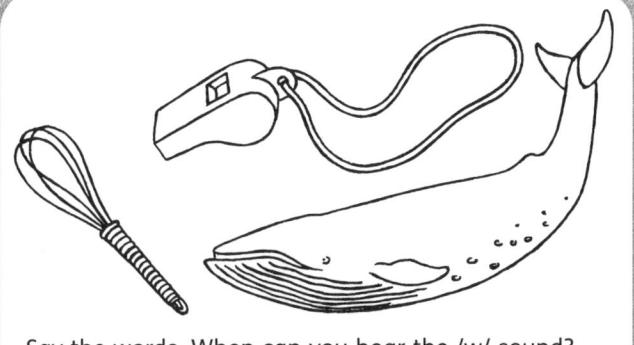

Say the words. When can you hear the /w/ sound?

Draw something beginning with **wh**.

sh th -ng -dge -ve **wh**

Practise your reading and writing

Spell and write words with the focus grapheme.

1. When will Biff get a wish?

2. When shall I whisk and whizz up the eggs?

Blend to read the words and sentences.

Copy one of the sentences while saying the sounds of the words. Draw a picture to match the sentence.

Practise the sound

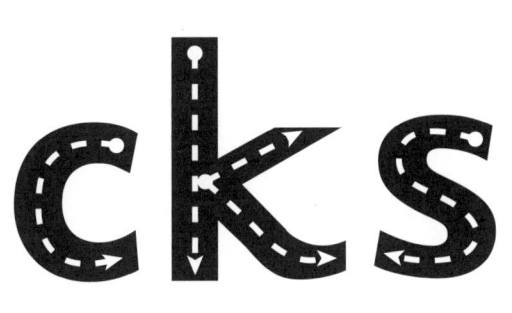

Say the sound. Trace the letters.

Say the word. Listen for the /ks/ sound.

six box wax mix fix tax

ox fox rocks packs licks

socks picks sticks bricks

Sound out and blend to read the words. Some words revise **x** and other words practise **cks**.

cks cks cks

Say the sound. Trace the letters. Write the letters.

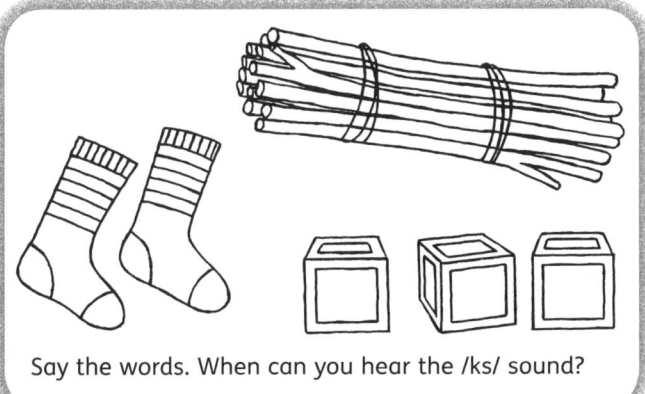

Say the words. When can you hear the /ks/ sound?

Draw something ending in **cks**.

th -ng -dge -ve wh **-cks**

Practise your reading and writing

Spell and write words with the focus grapheme.

1. He has six ducks that live in six shacks.

2. If they spot a fox, the ducks give six quacks, then we dash in and the fox backs off!

Blend to read the words and sentences.

Copy one of the sentences while saying the sounds of the words. Draw a picture to match the sentence.

Practise the sound

tch

Say the sound. Trace the letters.

Say the word. Listen for the /ch/ sound.

chess   chap   rich   much

hatch   latch   thatch   catch

patch   hutch   fetch   match

Sound out and blend to read the words. Some words revise **ch** and other words practise **tch**.

tch   tch   tch

Say the sound. Trace the letters. Write the letters.

Say the words. When can you hear the /ch/ sound?

Draw something ending in **tch**.

-ng   -dge   -ve   wh   -cks   **-tch**

Spell and write words with the focus grapheme.

1. The rabbit had lunch in his hutch.

2. A batch of chicks hatch, then they scratch at a patch of bugs.

Blend to read the words and sentences.

Copy one of the sentences while saying the sounds of the words. Draw a picture to match the sentence.

© Oxford University Press © Phonics International Ltd. 2020

Practise the sound

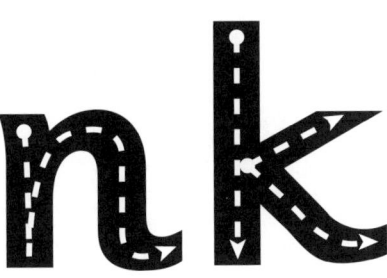

Say the sound. Trace the letters.

Say the word. Listen for the /ngk/ sound.

sing pong king sting wing

pink bank skunk sink blink

think thank drink blanket

Sound out and blend to read the words. Some words revise **ng** and other words practise **nk**.

nk nk nk nk

Say the sound. Trace the letters. Write the letters.

Say the words. When can you hear the /ngk/ sound?

Draw something ending in **nk**.

-ve wh -cks -tch -nk

Practise your reading and writing

Spell and write words with the focus grapheme.

1. I think I have a posh pink ring that fits me.

2. The king flings his drink and bangs on the gong!

Blend to read the words and sentences.

Copy one of the sentences while saying the sounds of the words. Draw a picture to match the sentence.

Say the sounds

y   sh   w

-zz   -x   th

th   ch   j   qu

-ng   v   z

-nk   wh   -dge

-tch   -cks   -ve

Oxford Reading Tree

Floppy's Phonics

Oxford Level 2

Activity Book 2

Say the sounds and practise your reading, spelling and handwriting skills.

Text © Oxford University Press
© Phonics International Ltd 2020

Illustrations by Oxford Designers and Illustrators

Cover Illustration by Alex Brychta

The characters in this work are the original creation of Roderick Hunt and Alex Brychta who retain copyright in the characters.

First published 2011
This edition published 2020

ISBN 978-1-38-200557-9

10
Printed in China

Paper used in the production of this book is a natural, recyclable product made from wood grown in sustainable forests. The manufacturing process conforms to the environmental regulations of the country of origin.

The manufacturer's authorised representative in the EU for product safety is Oxford University Press España S.A. of El Parque Empresarial San Fernando de Henares, Avenida de Castilla, 2 – 28830 Madrid (www.oup.es/en or product.safety@oup.com). OUP España S.A. also acts as importer into Spain of products made by the manufacturer.

Oxford OWL Helping your child's learning with free eBooks, essential tips and fun activities
www.oxfordowl.co.uk

OXFORD
UNIVERSITY PRESS
₹195

OXFORD
UNIVERSITY PRESS

How to get in touch:
web www.oxfordprimary.co.uk
email primary.enquiries@oup.com
tel. +44 (0) 1536 452610
fax +44 (0) 1865 313472

ISBN 978-1-38-200557-9

9 781382 005579